# The Ski Lesson

by Frances Ann Ladd

Illustrated by Duendes del Sur

SCHOLASTIC INC.
New York  Toronto  London  Auckland  Sydney
Mexico City  New Delhi  Hong Kong  Buenos Aires

Scooby and Shaggy
stood at the top
of a hill.
They looked scared.

They were taking
ski lessons!
"Skiing is a good sport!"
said the teacher.
"Skiing is a scary sport!"
said Shaggy.

"Let's go!"
said the teacher.
The teacher sped
down the hill.
Shaggy went first.
He skied down the slope.
He went as slow
as a snail.

Then Scooby
started skiing.
He went faster
and faster!
Scooby's scarf got stuck
in the skis!

"Stop, Scooby!"
Shaggy screamed.
Scooby skidded
to a stop!

His skis sprayed snow on Shaggy.
The snow was cold.
"Like, no more skiing," said Shaggy.

Shaggy swallowed a spoonful of sweet, steaming hot chocolate. "This is my idea of a good sport," he said.

Scooby smiled.
He spent the day
eating Scooby Snacks
instead of skiing.